Richard Scarry's

Best Word Book Ever

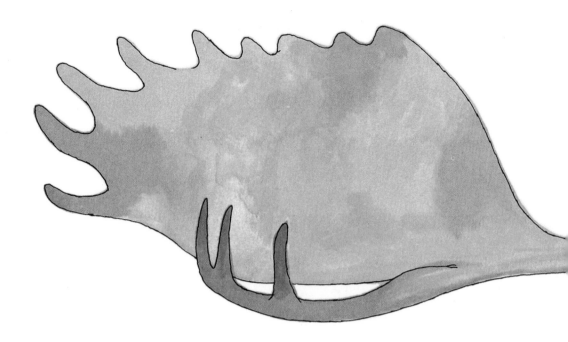

mosquito

First published in hardback in the UK by HarperCollins *Publishers* in 1980
This edition published by HarperCollins *Children's Books* in 2013

HarperCollins *Children's Books* is a division of HarperCollins *Publishers* Ltd,
77-85 Fulham Palace Road, London W6 8JB

1 3 5 7 9 10 8 6 4 2

ISBN: 978-0-00-750709-2

The HarperCollins website address is www.harpercollins.co.uk

Printed and bound in China.

moth

moose

Richard Scarry's
Best
Word Book
Ever

mouse

HarperCollins *Children's Books*

moss

mushroom

The Alphabet

The alligator is eating an apple.
The goose is wearing gloves.
What is the xiphias doing?

G goose

A alligator

B bear

H heart

I ice cream cone

C cat

J jacket

D dog

E egg

K kangaroo

F fish

L letter

M mailbag

N nut

O owl

P present

Q queen

R rug

S spider

T turtle

U umbrella

V vase

W walrus

X xiphias

xylophone

Y yarn

Z zip

curtains

sun

window

The New Day

It is the morning of a new day.
The sun is shining.
Kenny Bear gets up out of bed.

flannel

soap

towel

First he washes his
face and hands.

toothbrush

toothpaste

Then he brushes
his teeth.

mirror

comb

pyjamas

He combs his hair.

shirt

trousers

He dresses himself.

He makes his bed.

He goes to the kitchen
to eat his breakfast.

Kenny Bear sits in
his favourite chair.

He is very hungry.
This is what he eats —

cold fruit juice

warm cereal

with milk

pancakes

with butter and maple syrup

He doesn't
eat the
toaster.

fried eggs

bacon

toast

muffins

honey

jam

hot chocolate

cool milk

and a waffle.

When he finishes eating breakfast he
helps wash and dry the dishes.

cup

saucer

plate

bowl

fork

knife

spoon

tumbler

lid

jar

jug

frying pan

saucepan

pan

bottle

**juice
squeezer**

glass

Now he is ready to play with his friends.

The Rabbit Family's House

Father Rabbit, Mother Rabbit and the Rabbit children are getting ready for the new day. Their friend Owl is waiting for the children to come outside. Can you find him?

chimney

roof

mirror

lamp

bed

Big Brother's bedroom

cupboard

dining room

table

kitchen

sink

Father

back door

cooker

chair

floor

axe

Mother

woodpile

lawn

birdbath

smoke

WHOO

owl

aerial

light switch

television

record player

foot stool

Mickey

bunk bed

Molly

bathroom

bedroom

landing

front door

living room

candle

outside light

picture

telephone

fireplace

stairs

sofa or couch

hall

doormat

rug

window

stone path

Painting and Drawing with Colours

Painting and drawing are fun. You can use bright colours. You can paint with brushes or even your fingers. You can draw with crayons or pencils. What do you like to draw?

finger painting

paper

pencil

eraser

pencil drawing

make orange

make green

make grey

make purple

make pink

make brown

water dish

watercolours

poster paint

smock

paintbrushes

crayons

pastels

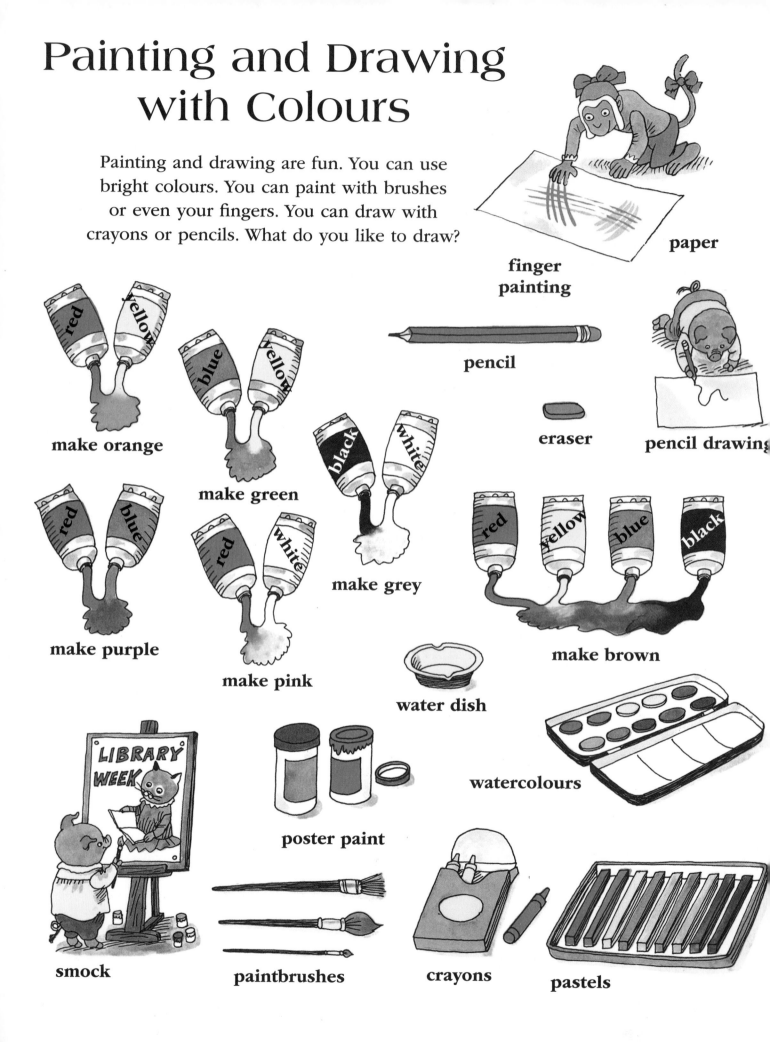

Toys

Sometimes it is fun to play by
yourself. Sometimes it is fun to
play with your friends.
What are your favourite toys?
Do you like to play with blocks?

rocking horse

tricycle

electric train set

truck and loader

blocks

scooter

glider

robot

building set

croquet

At the Playground

The children are all having fun doing different things. Which children are doing the things you like best?

seesaw

slide

leapfrog

hide-and-seek

somersault

ring a ring o'roses

skipping rope

ladder

rings

swing

sliding pole

top

roller skates

bubble blowing

kite

climbing frame

merry-go-round

tag

ring toss

hoop rolling

jacks

marbles

sandpit

kite string

bouncing ball

hopscotch

Tools

hammer

nail

Everyone is very busy working with tools. What tools do you have in your house? What would you like to build?

pushpin

axe

ladder

log

carpenter

board

saw

sawdust

sandpaper

hacksaw

drill

plane

woodpecker

vice

jigsaw

wood shavings

screwdriver

screws

pliers

file

bucksaw

trowel

bricklayer

hoe

brick   brick wall   cement

timber

fence
painter

paintbrush

sawhorse   ball of string

paint

ruler   barrel

tack   tack hammer   axe

folding ruler

toolbox

penknife

square

putty knife   shovel

bolt   nut

dirt

monkey
wrench

compass   wheelbarrow

pick

glue

haystack

cow

apple tree

farmhouse

water pump

meadow

nce

sheep

horse

clothesline

apple

grass

clothes basket

Kenny Bear is going to feed the chickens.

The Bears' Farm

The Bears are working hard on their farm. What are they all doing? What is the duck doing? What is the scarecrow supposed to be doing? He is not doing it, is he?

chicken coop

well

duck pond

duck

ducklings

bee

pitchfork

beehive

weather
instruments

blimp

microphone

control tower

helicopter

At the Airport

The air traffic controller is talking to the pilot
of the jet passenger plane. The controller is
giving the pilot take-off instructions.

baggage train

waiting
room

tourist

binoculars

camera

observation deck

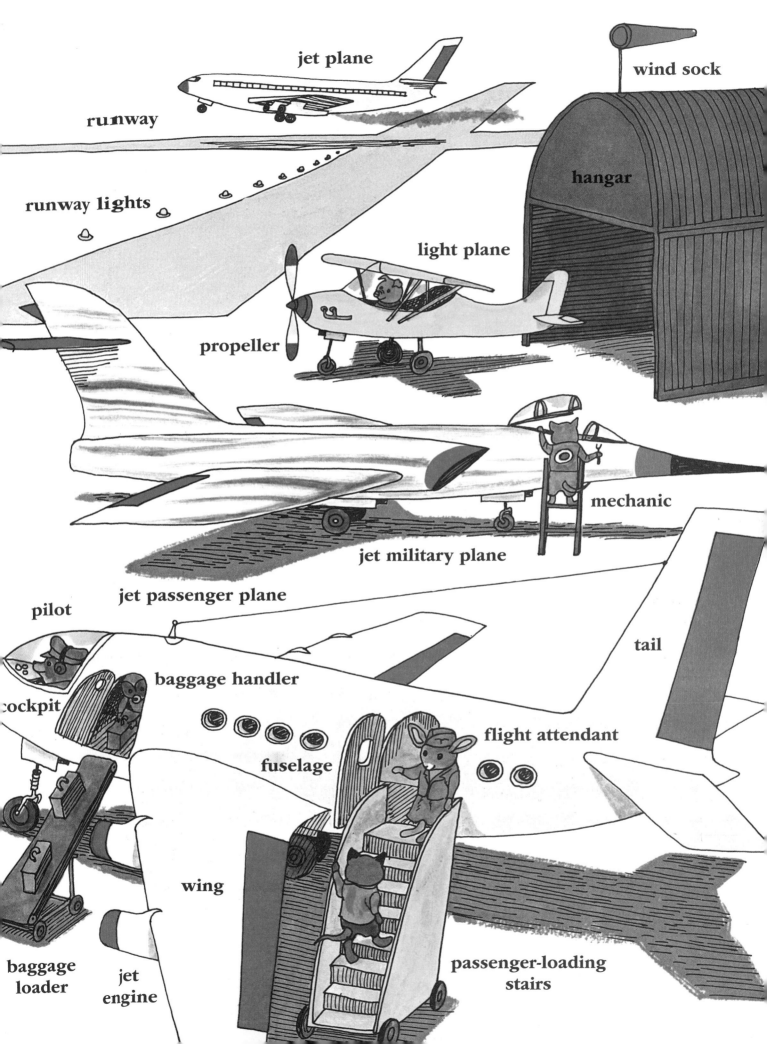

meat cleaver

hook

saw

ham

MEATS

scales

brown paper

string

pickle barrel

butcher

salami

sausages

mince

rubbish bin

bacon

chop

fish

steak

a piglet who wants to work in the supermarket when she grows up

trolley

sawdust

At the Supermarket

The Pigs are buying groceries for their family.
What would you like to buy the next time
you go to the supermarket?
Would you like to buy a pickle?

shopper

books

BOOKS ARE FUN!

customer

orange juice

raisins

money

purse

eggs

milk

cashier

ice cream

butter

till

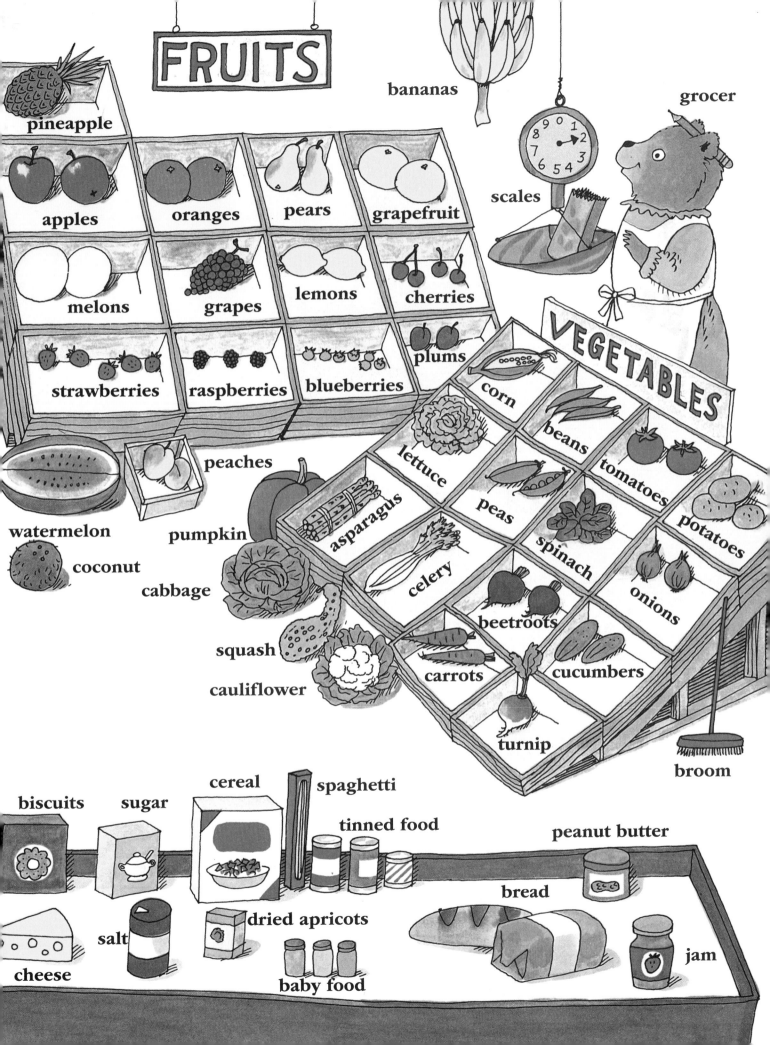

FRUITS

pineapple

bananas

grocer

apples

oranges

pears

grapefruit

scales

melons

grapes

lemons

cherries

strawberries

raspberries

blueberries

plums

peaches

watermelon

pumpkin

coconut

cabbage

VEGETABLES

corn

lettuce

beans

tomatoes

asparagus

peas

potatoes

celery

spinach

squash

beetroots

onions

cauliflower

carrots

cucumbers

turnip

broom

biscuits

sugar

cereal

spaghetti

tinned food

peanut butter

bread

cheese

salt

dried apricots

jam

baby food

Meal time

The Pig family is having
a special celebration meal.
There is so much good
food to enjoy!
What do you see on the
table that you like to eat?

carving knife and fork

roast beef

meat platter

coffeepot

tablespoon

salt shaker

teapot

pepper pot

fork

dinner plate

glass

cream jug

knife

spoon

saucer

cup

napkin

sugar bowl

turkey

cake

milk jug

baked potatoes

green beans

jelly

cranberry sauce

pumpkin mash

onions

mashed potatoes

beetroots

ice cream

peas

butter

steak

soup

pie

salad

white bread

brown bread

rolls

smokestack

submarine

stern

bow

ocean liner

police boat

barge

tugboat

pirate ship

ferry

Boats and Ships

One of the things in the water is not a boat, but it helps boats to find the place they want to go. Do you know what it is?

motorboat

paddle

canoe

kayak

oar

rowing boat

freighter

lightship

AMBROSE

CG-7

coast guard ship

F.D.

fireboat

oil tanker

fishing nets

sport-fishing boat

fishing trawler

10

speedboat

houseboat

raft

THE WHITE SWAN

2

sailing boat

light buoy

Keeping Healthy

Your doctor and your dentist are your good friends.
They want you to stay healthy and strong.
Will you give your doctor and dentist a big smile the next
time you see them? How big a smile can you smile?

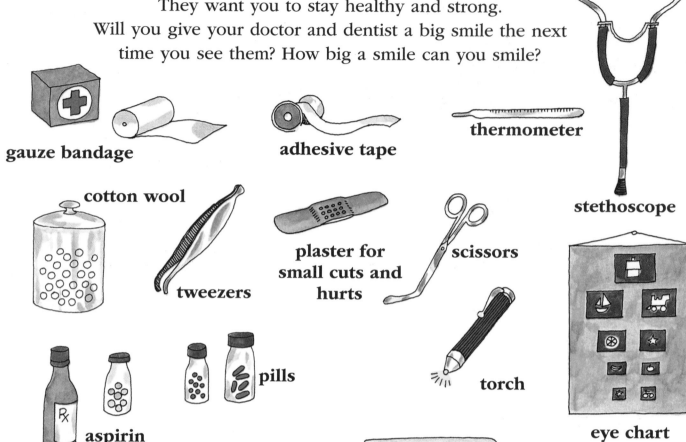

gauze bandage

adhesive tape

thermometer

cotton wool

tweezers

plaster for small cuts and hurts

scissors

stethoscope

medicine

aspirin

pills

torch

eye chart

rubber hammer to make legs kick

tongue depressor for looking down throats

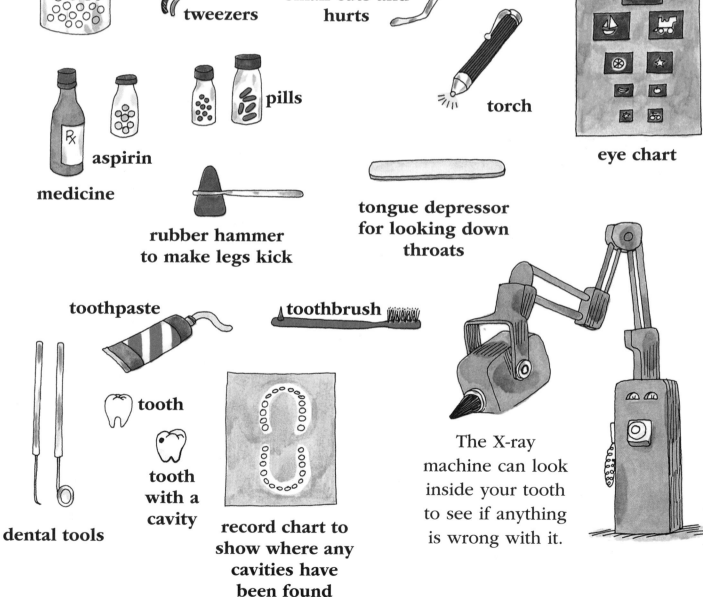

toothpaste

toothbrush

tooth

tooth with a cavity

dental tools

record chart to show where any cavities have been found

The X-ray machine can look inside your tooth to see if anything is wrong with it.

The doctor listens to your heart.

scales

hurt tail

doctor

patient

optician

The optician
tests your eyes.

dental unit

inse
owl

instrument table

water cup

dentist

dentist's chair

dental hygienist

The dentist looks for cavities and
the dental hygienist explains how
to care for your teeth.

The Bear Twins Get Dressed

Kenny Bear wakes up one cold, frosty morning.
He wants to dress very warmly before going outside.
He yawns and gets up out of bed. He takes off his
pyjamas, folds them, and puts them in a drawer.

What should he wear today to keep warm?

slippers

pyjama top

pyjama bottoms

trousers

He puts on his

T-shirt   underpants   cap   shirt   dungarees

tie   jumper   socks   hat   scarf   trainers   gloves

jacket   overcoat   raincoat   and rainhat.

As Kenny is walking out of the
front door his father says,
"Don't forget to put your boots on!"

boots

Kathy Bear stretches hard before she gets out of bed. She takes off her nightdress and hangs it on the hook in her wardrobe.

What do you think Kathy should wear today to keep warm?

nightdress

She puts on her

 **pants**

 **vest**

 hair ribbon

 **blouse**   **skirt**

 jumper

socks

ear muffs

 **shoes**

 **snowsuit**

and mittens

She puts her purse

 **into her backpack.**

As Kathy is walking out of the front door her mother says, "Don't forget to put your boots on!"

Do you ever forget to put on your boots?

deer

lion

elephant

tiger

panda

monkeys

polar bear

brown bear

gorilla

buffalo

camel

zebra

fish

zookeeper

giraffe

leopard

sea lion

zoo train

At the Zoo

The vet makes sure all the animals are healthy.

Mr. and Mrs. Mouse took their children to the zoo. How will the children ever be able to get all those balloons into their house tonight? Which is your favourite animal at the zoo?

rhinoceros

hippopotamus

balloon seller

BOOK PUBLISHER

COSTUMES

skyscraper

aerial

church

NEWSPAPER OFFICE

Dancing School

traffic lights

flats

Bookshop

CHEMIST

telephone box

postbox

book reader

street

In the City

postman

post van

Mouse has just bought a book from the bookshop.
She is going to buy a newspaper and then join
her rabbit friends at the café and drink some
lemonade with them. Show with your finger the
way she will go. Remember to have her look
both ways before she crosses a road.

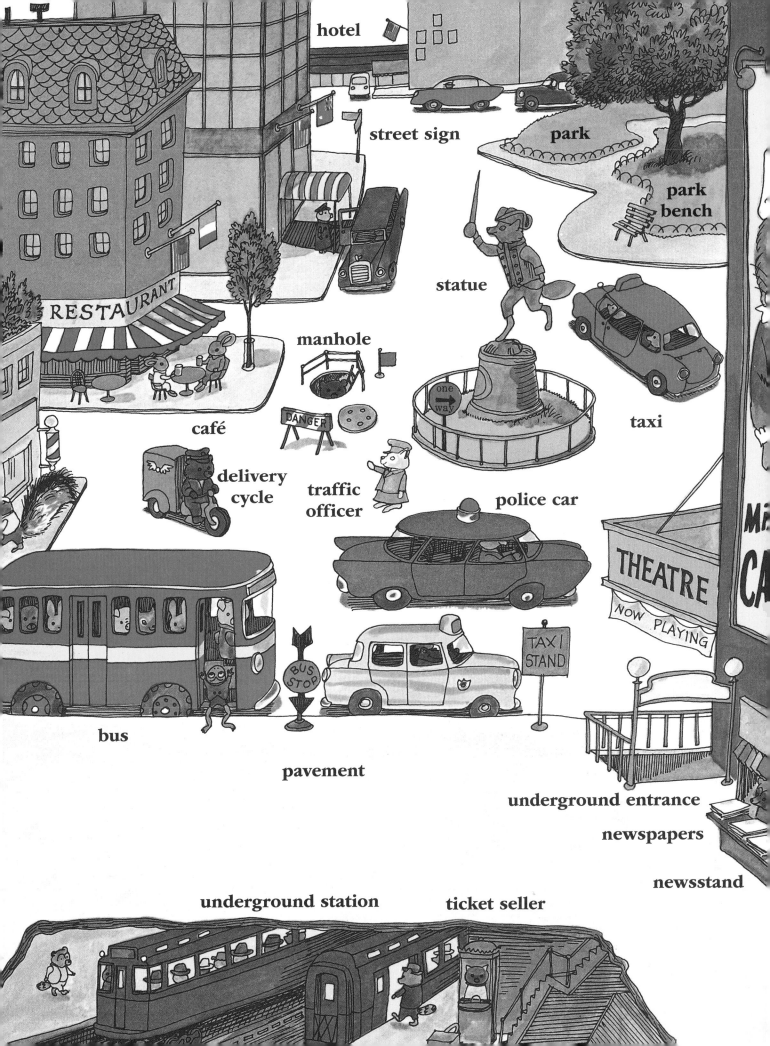

hotel

street sign

park

park bench

statue

taxi

manhole

RESTAURANT

DANGER

café

delivery cycle

traffic officer

police car

THEATRE

NOW PLAYING

MR CA

TAXI STAND

BUS STOP

bus

pavement

underground entrance

newspapers

newsstand

underground station

ticket seller

A Drive in the Country

radio tower

There are many things to see when
you take a drive in the country.
Can you see Harry and Sally, the mountain
climbers? Can you see what Harry has
dropped from his backpack?

island

ocean

factory

petrol
station

lake

tunnel

petrol
pump

motorway

tollbooth

bridge

farm

brook

mill

stream

waterfall

picnic area

picnickers

lighthouse

fire lookout tower

beach

crane

bay

woods

seaport

drawbridge

hill

tug

mountain

windmill

village

river

pond

log cabin

mountain climbers

cliff

road

forest

backpack

apple

Holidays

Holidays are happy times, aren't they?
Which holiday do you like best?
I bet you like them all.
On holidays we visit friends and relatives.
Sometimes we give or get presents.
What would you like to get for your birthday?

New Year's Day

St. Valentine's Day

Easter

horn

valentine

Easter egg

Easter bunny

Easter chick

Birthday

balloons

rattle

cake

ice cream

Halloween

moon

ghost

witch

skeleton

black cat

witch's broom

pumpkin

trick-or-treat bag

Hanukkah

angel

menorah

candle

wreath

Christmas

Christmas tree

stockings

holly

decorations

tree lights

beard

fireplace

Father Christmas

sack

present

At School

School is fun. There are so many things we learn to do. Kathy Bear is learning how to find a lost mitten.

pencil

fountain pen

pencil sharpener

ballpoint pen

paper

chalk

straw

ink

notebook

blackboard eraser

eraser

milk

cookies

scissors

string

yarn

paper clip

glue

workbook

storybook

drawing pins

modelling clay

lost-clothing drawer

flag

clock

bell

blackboard

calendar

teacher

a b c

cat dog

JANUARY
1 2 3 4
5 6 7 8 9 10 11
12 13 14 15 16 17 18
19 20 21 22 23 24 25
26 27 28 29 30 31

inkwell

map

map stand

wastepaper
basket

artist

pupil

desk

classroom

music
teacher

paper shapes

My
name
is Pig

1 2 3
4 5 6

cupboard

feather duster

dustpan

mop

broom

vacuum cleaner

egg timer

shelf

cooker hood

Mother Pig

coffeepot

kettle

oven

iron

In the Kitchen

All the Pigs like to work in the kitchen.
They are making good things to eat.
What is Father Pig making?
What is Mother Pig putting into the oven?

ironing board

teaspoon

tablespoon

soup spoon

double boiler

blender

pestle

toaster

mortar

saucepan

corkscrew

ladle

colander

cutting board

measuring spoons

matches

potato masher

salt shaker

pepper grinder

electric mixer

cookery book

carving fork and knife

When You Grow Up

What would you like to be when you are bigger?
Would you like to be a chef?
Would you like to be a doctor or a nurse?
What would you like to be?

police officer

firefighter

sailor

nurse

taxi driver

farmer

gardener

doctor

carpenter

musician

scientist

baker

dentist

secretary

chef

singer

artist

pilot

angler

truck driver

teacher

garage mechanic

judge

reporter

photographer

shopkeeper

librarian

dancer

daddy

mummy

ings We Do

There are many things that we can do.
And there are some things we cannot do.
What is the one thing we can't do?
Look and see.

dig

blow

build

break

sleep

wake up

walk

run

stand

sit

read

watch

draw and write

pull

push

kick

talk

listen

shout

whisper

eat

laugh

smile

cry

drink

jump over

crawl under

fall down

we can't fly

peek

go up

go down

tip a hat

go in

come out

Work Machines

Busy, busy, busy bears. Most of the bears
are busy moving dirt with their machines.
But there is one bear who has a machine
which does something else to the dirt.
Which bear is it? What is she doing?

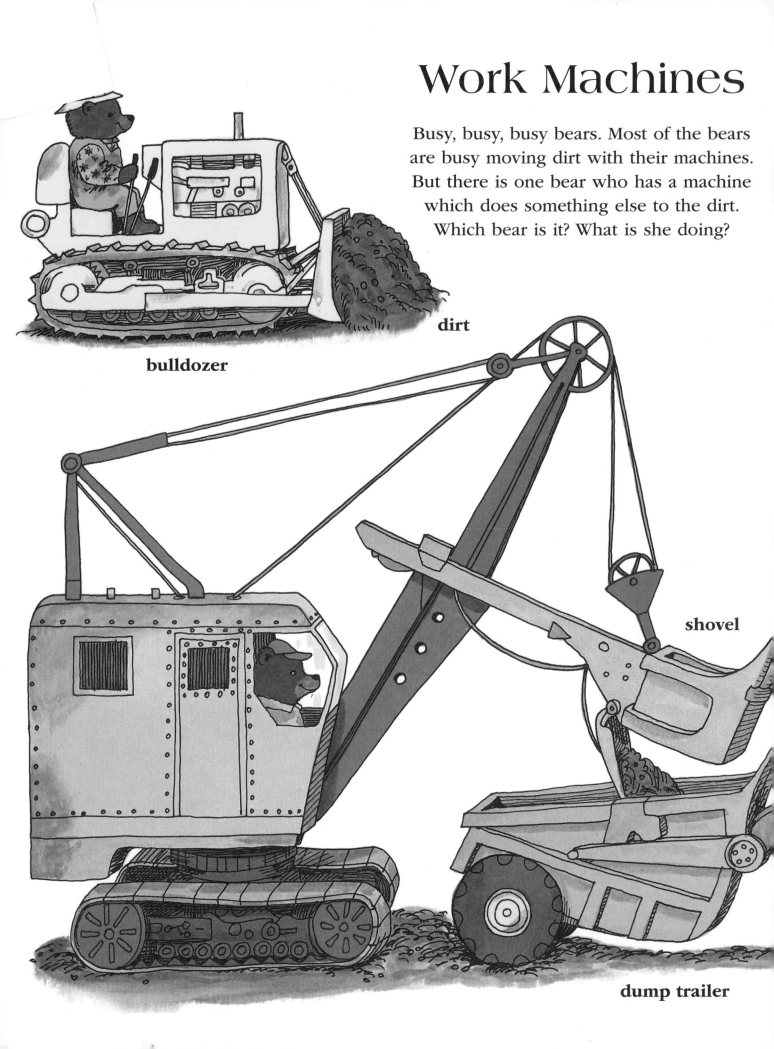

dirt

bulldozer

shovel

dump trailer

tractor scraper

dump truck

tractor shovel

bucket loader

dirt

and tractor

smooth dirt

roller

rough dirt

car transporter

petrol truck

milk van

broken-down car

tow truck

motorcycle

taxi

sports car

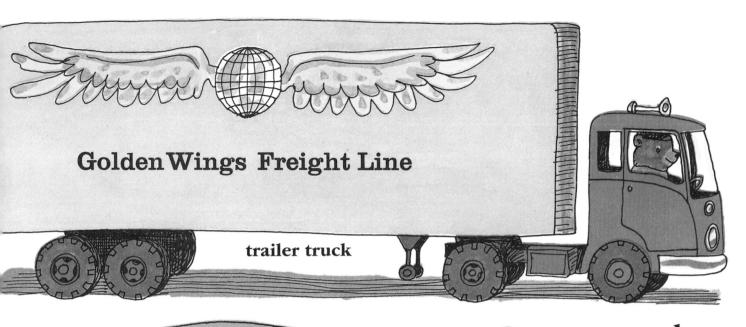

GoldenWings Freight Line

trailer truck

Cars and Trucks

Down the street go the cars and trucks. But look! Some of the cars don't have drivers. Which cars have no drivers?

rubbish truck

boat trailer

saloon car

motor scooter

vintage car

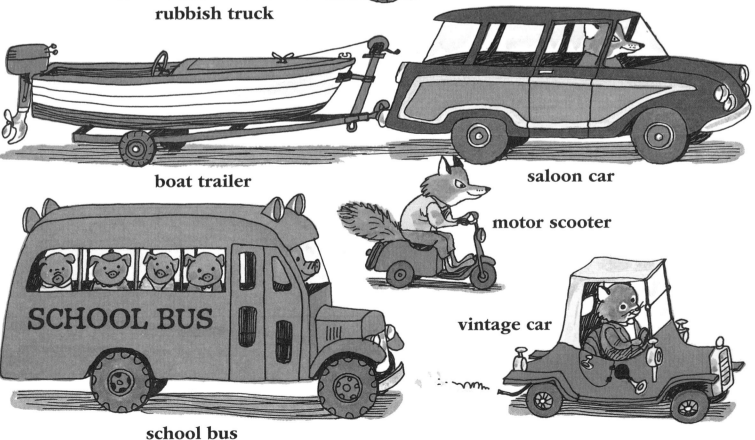

school bus

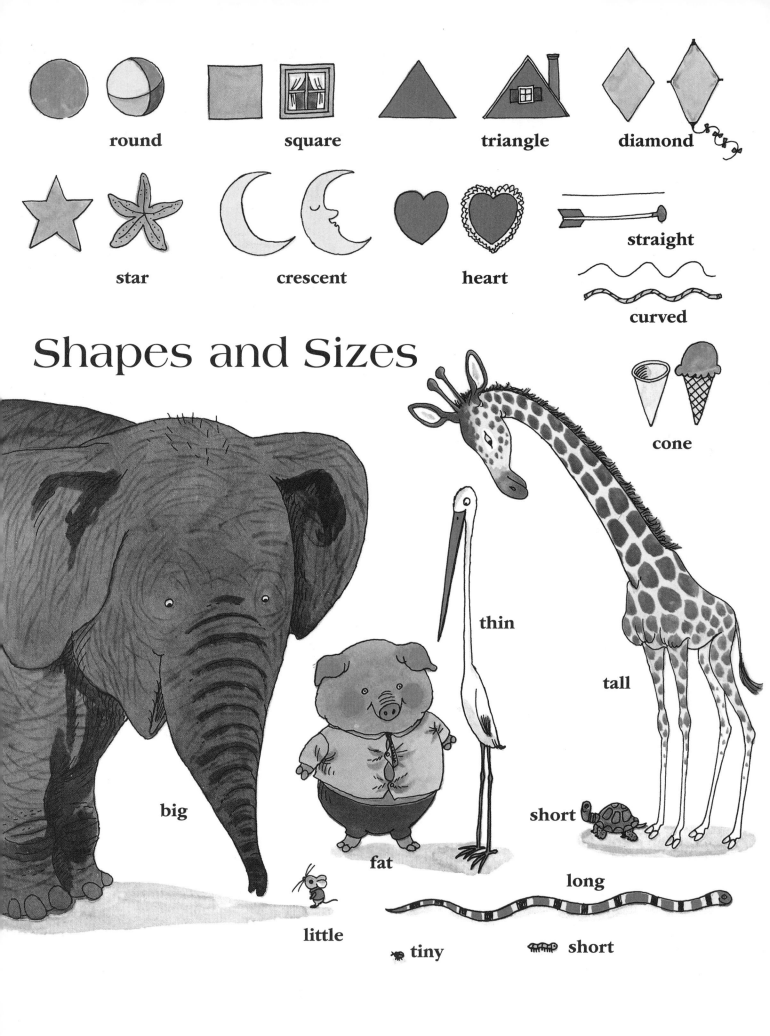

round

square

triangle

diamond

star

crescent

heart

straight

curved

Shapes and Sizes

cone

thin

tall

big

short

fat

long

little

tiny

short

father   mother

The Baby

The Cat family has a new baby kitten.
They don't know what to name it.
What would you like to
name the new baby?
Write the kitten's name here.

__ __ __ __ __ __

grandmother

uncle

bottle

baby

rattle

brother

nappy

sister

aunt

grandfather

playpen

cousin

high chair

pushchair

cot

Moses
basket

play table

walker

buggy

At the Circus

The band is playing and the animals are doing their acts.
What do you like to watch best at the circus?

tent pole

balancing pole

tightrope performer

tightrope

band

horse rider

rope ladder

bandstand

circus horse

elephant

sawdust

ring

trick dog

clown

ringmaster

flag

circus tent

trapeze

trapeze artist

safety net

acrobat

ticket seller

hoop

lion

cage

lion tamer

juggler

sea lion

popcorn seller

balloon seller

The Firefighters to the Rescue

Will the brave firefighters put out the fire in time? I think so, don't you?

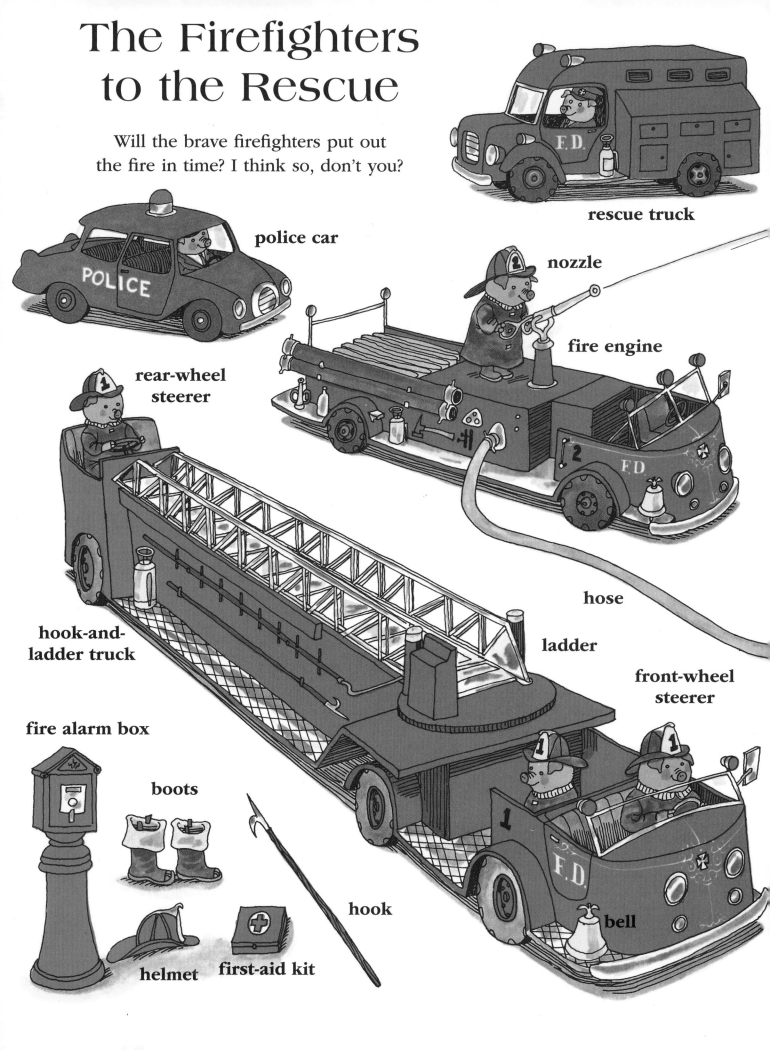

rescue truck

police car

nozzle

fire engine

rear-wheel steerer

hose

hook-and-ladder truck

ladder

front-wheel steerer

fire alarm box

boots

hook

bell

helmet

first-aid kit

ambulance

flames

water

smoke

fire chief

megaphone

cat in danger

fire chief's car

firefighter

pumper

fire hydrant

ladder

firefighters

rescue net

firefighter

fire extinguisher

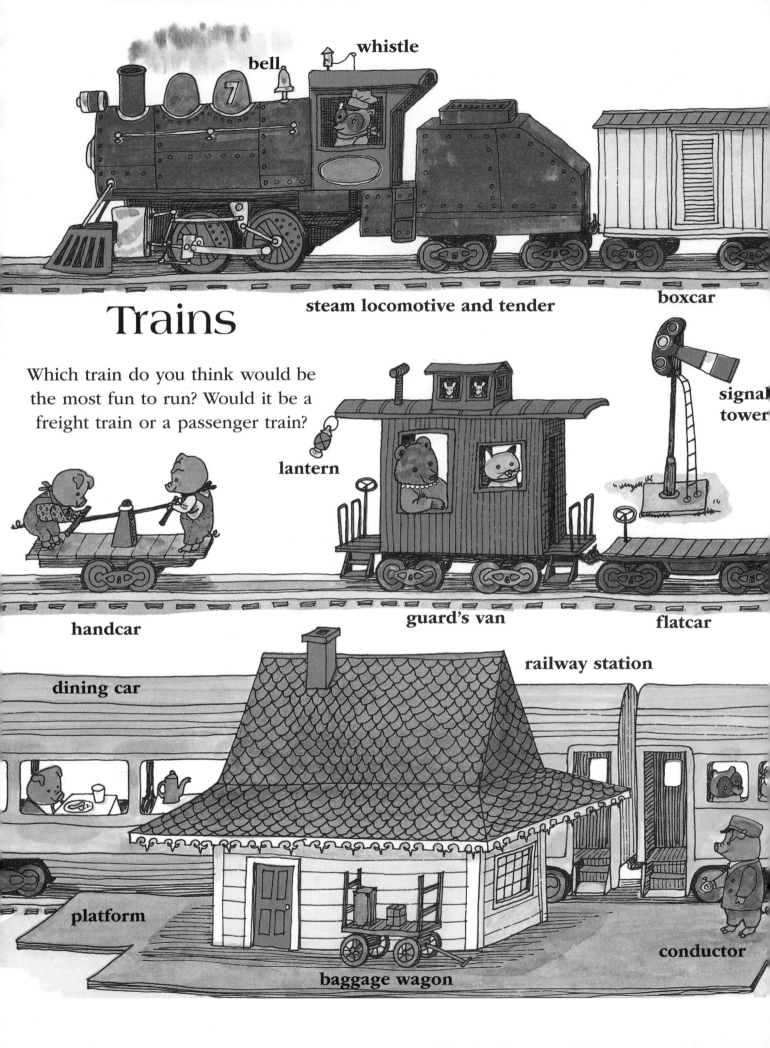

bell

whistle

Trains

steam locomotive and tender

boxcar

Which train do you think would be the most fun to run? Would it be a freight train or a passenger train?

lantern

signal tower

handcar

guard's van

flatcar

dining car

railway station

platform

baggage wagon

conductor

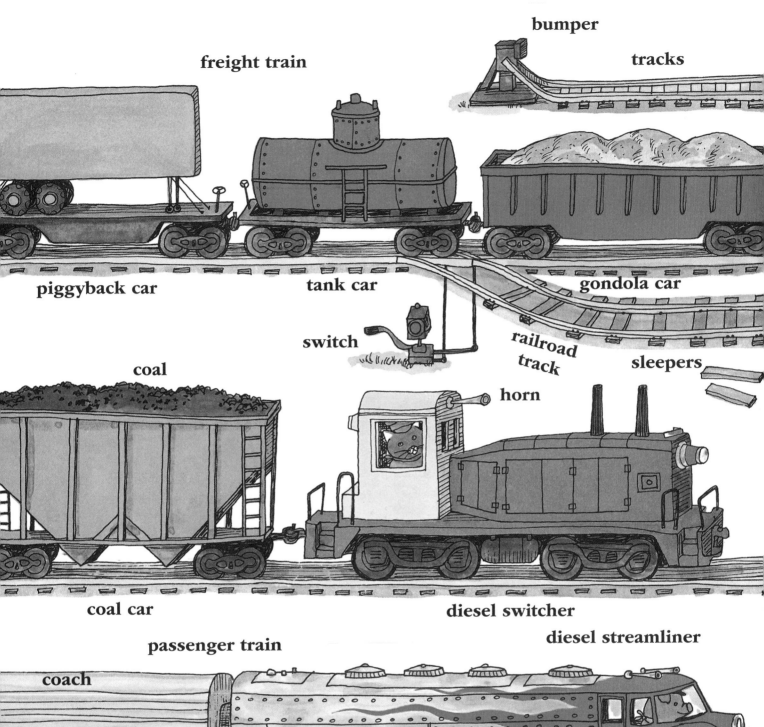

bumper

tracks

freight train

piggyback car

tank car

gondola car

switch

railroad track

sleepers

coal

horn

coal car

diesel switcher

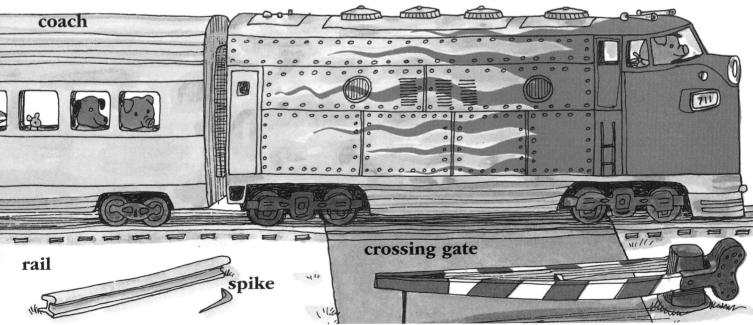

passenger train

diesel streamliner

coach

crossing gate

rail

spike

At the Beach

In the summertime it is fun to go to the beach. What do you think Rabbit hears in the seashell? Is it the sound of the waves?

telescope

lighthouse

oar

anchor

beach toy

spade

rowing boat

sandpiper

sand castle

skate

bluefish

oyster

lobster

scallop

hermit crab

clam

Making Things Grow

Everyone is working in the garden.
Mr. Crow has a seed in his mouth.
Do you think he will plant it?
Or will he eat it?

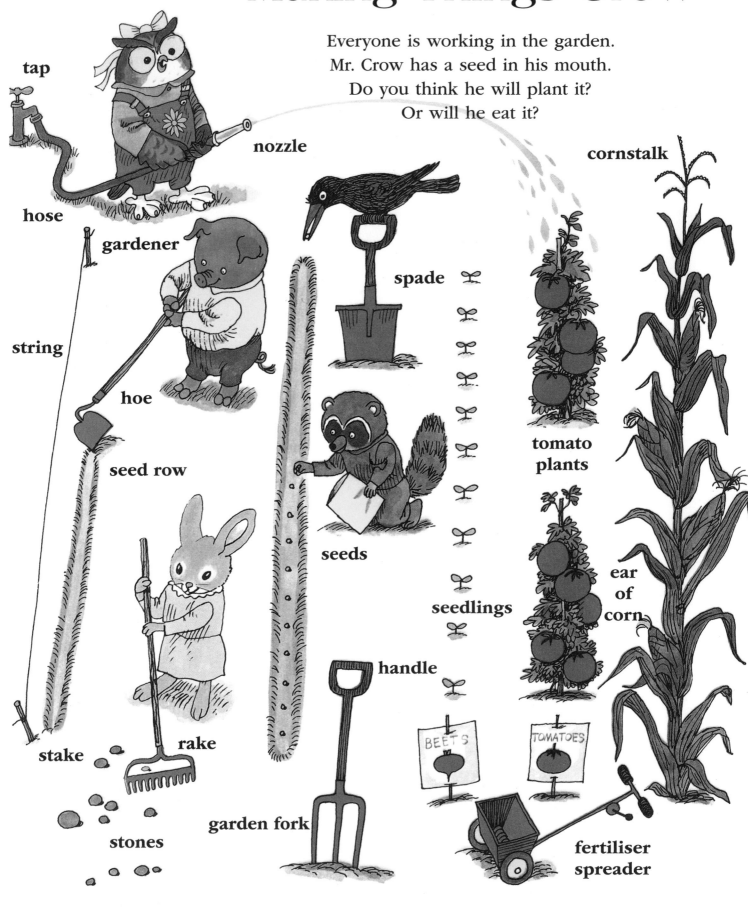

tap

nozzle

cornstalk

hose

gardener

spade

string

hoe

seed row

tomato plants

seeds

ear of corn

seedlings

stake

rake

handle

BEETS

TOMATOES

stones

garden fork

fertiliser spreader

The Weather

When we go outdoors we see what the weather is like. Sometimes it is sunny. Sometimes it is cloudy. It can be windy, or cold, or hot. It can be snowing or raining. What was the weather like outdoors today? What is your favourite kind of weather?

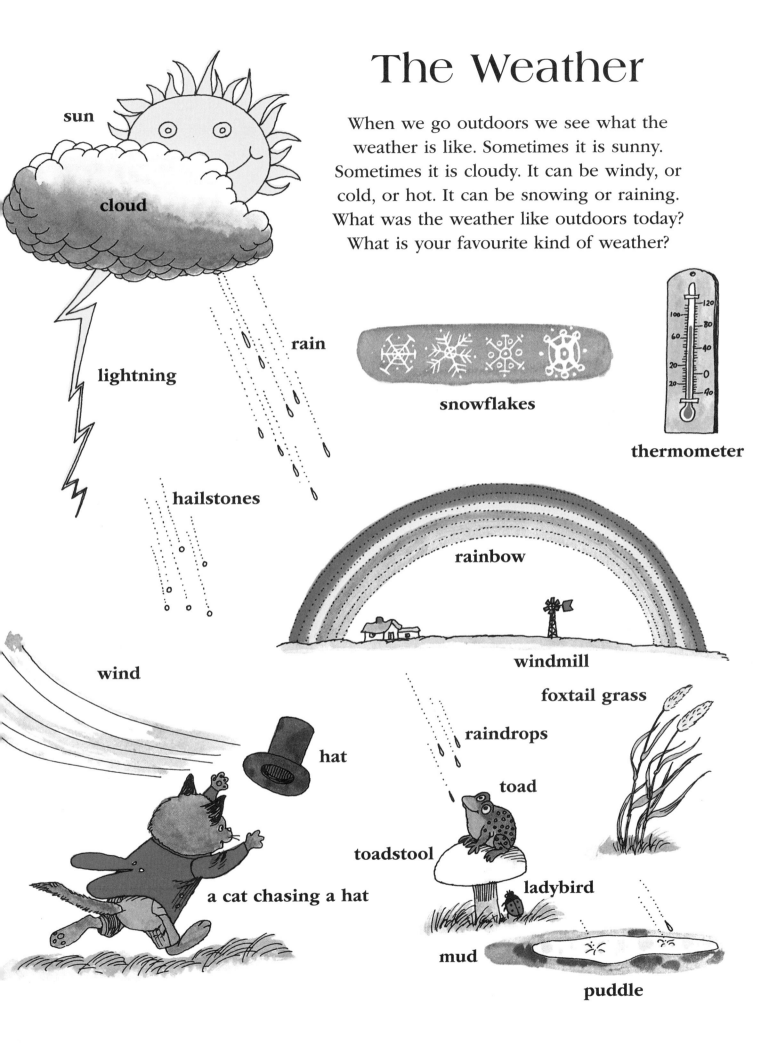

sun

cloud

lightning

rain

hailstones

snowflakes

thermometer

rainbow

windmill

wind

hat

foxtail grass

raindrops

toad

toadstool

ladybird

a cat chasing a hat

mud

puddle

kite

rain shower

plough

buds   robin

nest

Spring

Look at that baby lamb hop!
It is spring. She is happy.
Look at Mr. Bear coming out of his cave!
It is spring. He is happy.
Now he can use his new lawn mower.

tree

lamb

bush

bridge

brook

cave

fern

roots

turtle

frog

pussy willow

daffodils

lawn mower

crocus

violets

cow

meadow

calf

cornfield

fence

Summer

Do you like to go on picnics
in the summertime?
Ants just love to go to picnics.
Do you know why?

car

tent

fly

barbeque

screen

charcoal

picnic basket cooler

hamburger

ketchup

charcoal bag

hotdog

mosquito

pole

paper cup

mustard

pickle

rock

ants

float

cattails

frog

deck

pond

water lily

dragonfly

pebbles

stones

sun

duck

falling leaves

corn stock

stone wall

pumpkin

nuts

gate

roadside stand

apple juice

corn

jam

Autumn

In the autumn the air gets colder. The green leaves turn to bright colours. Then they fall to the ground.

squash

smoke

basket of apples

turkey

flames

rake

bonfire

leaves

Winter

There are many ways to have fun on the snow and ice. Maybe you would like to do all of them. Would you?

snowstorm

sleigh

icicle

fishing shack

ice fishing

skis

sledge

toboggan

snow

ice-skating rink

ice skater

snowball

hockey stick

puck

ice skates

scarf

spare tyre

jeep

snowplough

a pig all wrapped up

snowman

Little Things

Here are many little things.
What little things do you sometimes
put on your bedroom wall?

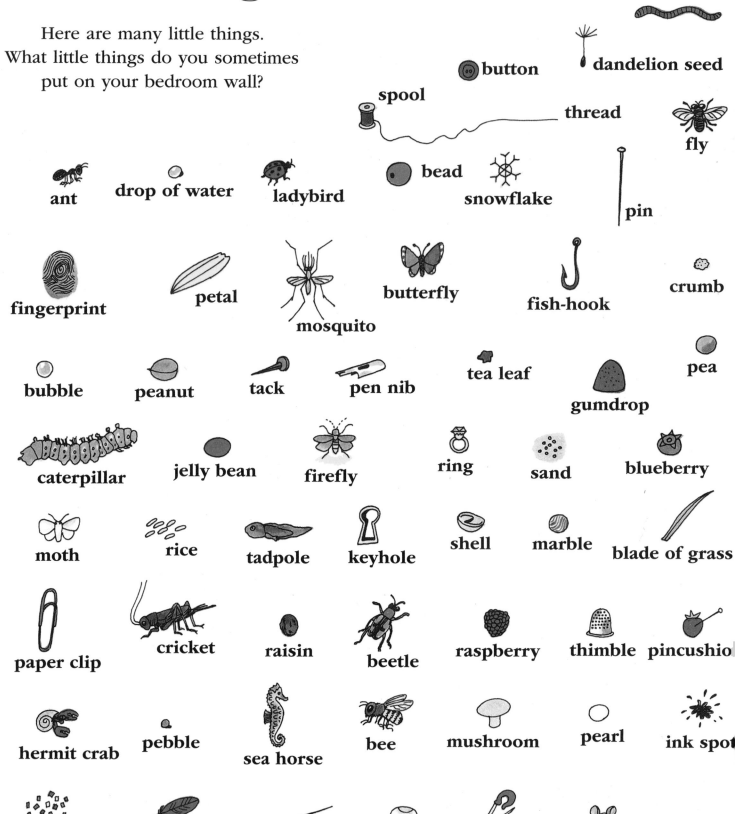

worm

button

dandelion seed

spool

thread

fly

ant   drop of water   ladybird   bead   snowflake

pin

fingerprint   petal   mosquito   butterfly   fish-hook   crumb

bubble   peanut   tack   pen nib   tea leaf   gumdrop   pea

caterpillar   jelly bean   firefly   ring   sand   blueberry

moth   rice   tadpole   keyhole   shell   marble   blade of grass

paper clip   cricket   raisin   beetle   raspberry   thimble   pincushio

hermit crab   pebble   sea horse   bee   mushroom   pearl   ink spot

confetti   feather   splinter   bean   safety pin   dot

baby mouse

Parts of the Body

Bears use their paws to pick things up.
What do you use?

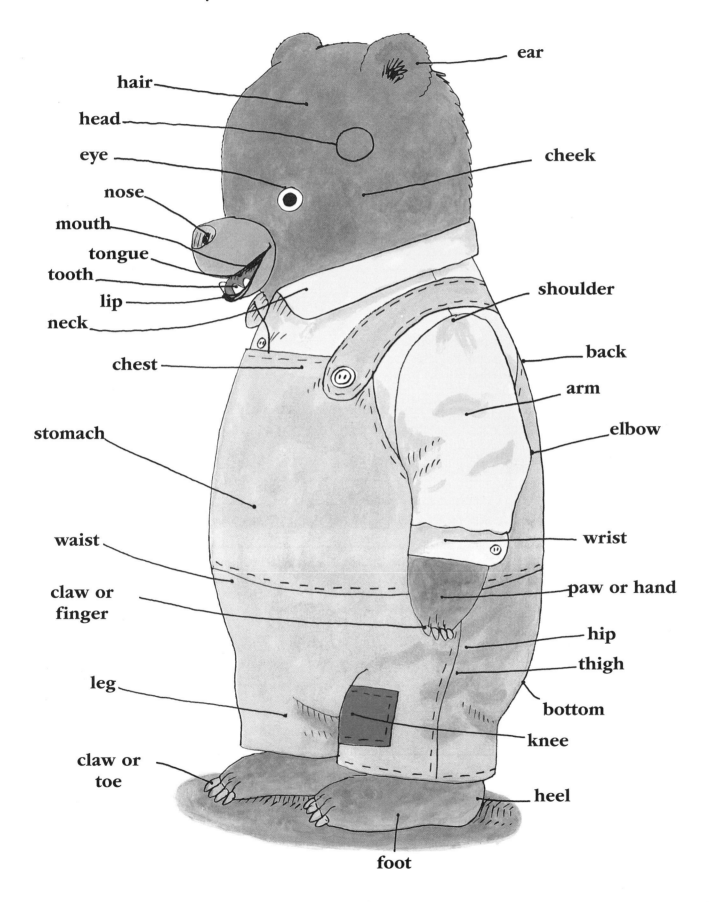

ear

hair

head

eye

cheek

nose

mouth

tongue

tooth

lip

neck

shoulder

back

arm

chest

elbow

stomach

waist

wrist

claw or
finger

paw or hand

hip

thigh

leg

bottom

knee

claw or
toe

heel

foot

Bedtime

Little Elephant is getting ready for bed.
But who is that hiding under the bed?
Find that rascal and tell her to brush
her teeth and get ready for bed, too.

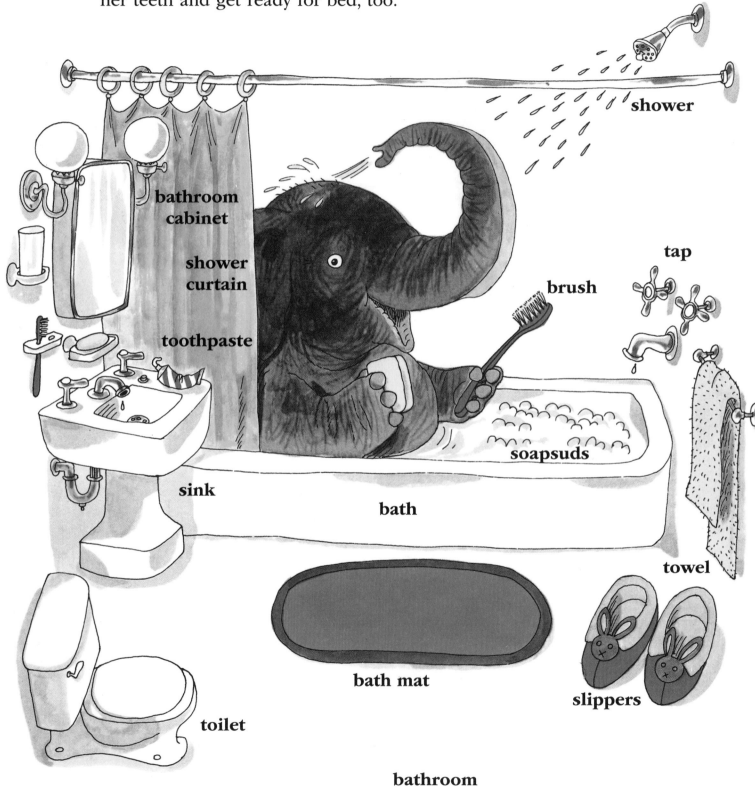

shower

bathroom
cabinet

shower
curtain

tap

brush

toothpaste

soapsuds

sink

bath

towel

bath mat

slippers

toilet

bathroom

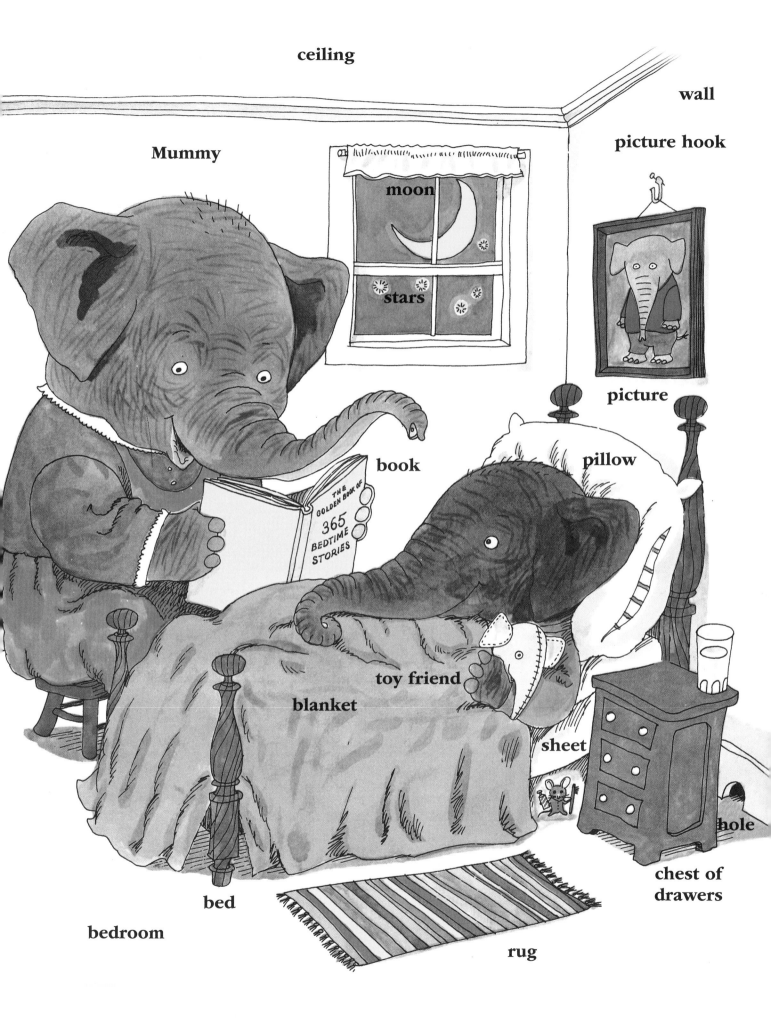

Numbers

How high can you count?
Can you count up to twenty ladybirds?
I'll bet you can.

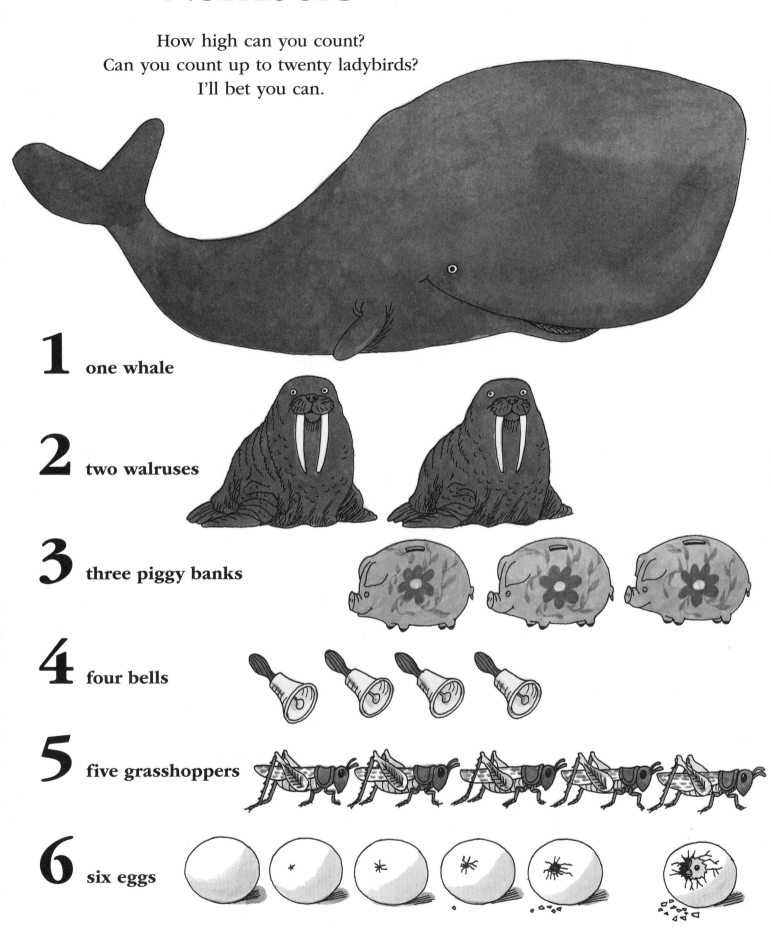

1 one whale

2 two walruses

3 three piggy banks

4 four bells

5 five grasshoppers

6 six eggs

7 seven caterpillars

8 eight spools

9 nine spiders

10 ten keys

11 eleven ants

12 twelve rings

13 thirteen gumdrops

14 fourteen leaves

15 fifteen snowflakes

16 sixteen acorns

17 seventeen pins

18 eighteen buttons

19 nineteen beads

20 twenty ladybirds

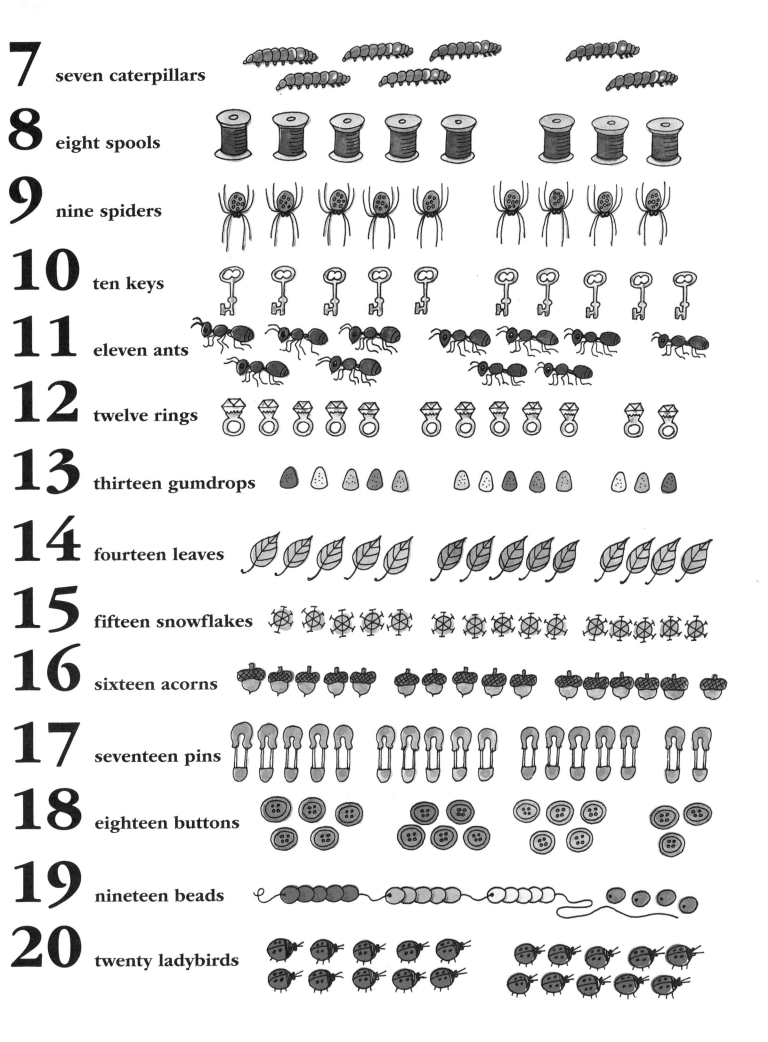